The Dark Side of the Blue Line
by
Nicholas Ruggiero

ISBN: 978-1-09839-133-1

Dedication

This book is dedicated to the men and woman that keep the thin blue line thriving and protect us without hesitation.

I would like to thank my daughter Hailey for keeping me grounded and reminding me that I'm still somebody. To my daughter Emily who over the past year has faced adversity and found her true self. I'm proud of both of you.

To my wife who's my hero and savior for showing what forgiveness looks like and always pointing me north. I've been a broken man for a long time and you stuck with me even when I gave up on myself. I hope one day i can live up to the man you see before you.

Thank you to my parents for encouraging me and understanding my uniqueness. My mom for always encouraging me even when it's hard to do.

Thank you TJ for being my big brother and your encouragement means the world. Laura and Alex I'm blessed to have you in my life.

Thank you Mike Ferrante for being a brother from another mother and always being there no matter what. Michael and Joseph I'm proud of the men you're turning into. Lisa no one likes you…You'll never be in the club.

Glenny and Anna thank you for the encouragement and supporting the cafe.

Thank you; Sergeant John Crowley, Nick Hadley, Peacemaker Coffee, www.supremewhiskestones.com, @booksbehindthebadge, Cami Miller, Maddox & Madden, Debra Quarrey, Shaun Smith, Ernest Stevens, William Young, Ed Vogt (Thanks for the cigars and honesty), Cappuccino thank you for healing this broken man, Melanie for training Cappi and giving me the best service dog, Heather, Nathan, Hannah, Ella - @rocksforleos, Marco and Andrea for bringing NYC to VA, Loren for being a friend and awesome co-host, Marc Basye, Bart Whiting, Carla Witt, Thomas Harley, www.midnightplatoon.com, www.ferociousbeard.com, and www.rollcallroomcafe.com.

Forewords

When I first heard Nick speak, it was through my

headphones while I ran a 5K, my first mistake.

I had stumbled upon the show, The Roll Call Room

Podcast, while searching for a new police

related show to listen to.

As I rounded my last kilometer, Nick was regaling the

listeners with a story about a prank he had played on a

former supervisor. I nearly fell, tripping over my own

shoes, laughing as the cold wind blew.

This incident, of course, was happening during the 4th

week of the "2 Weeks to Flatten the Curve" in 2020. I

tried my best to keep the snot and other debris inside my

nose as I passed other citizens around our small town, who

I'm sure all thought that I was stricken with "The Sickness." I giggled and snorted my way through the last few

meters of my run that day.

I was hooked on the show, and soon enough, Nick and I touched base on social media. I reached out through my own public platform and we quickly became "friends" via the internet, sharing memes and other jokes about the job.

A few months went by and I was asked to be a guest on the show. I gladly accepted and will be forever grateful that I did. Through the conversation that we had on his show, available in the archives, we established a friendship that would quickly develop into a mentorship of sorts.

Although Nick may appear salty and disheveled on the outside, with the giant, un-groomed beard, not unlike that of a train-hopping hobo, he is very truly soft and squishy on the inside, and on the outside, too.

In all seriousness, Nick has done publicly what most men, and cops alike, are not willing to do privately. Speaking out about mental health awareness is tough enough, but telling your OWN story about it is another thing. Raw, unforgiving, and yes, a bit brash, Nick's delivery in his original book, available from Amazon in double spaced format with large print so it's easier for older commanders to read, Mental Health Barricade, was necessary. I found myself relating to many stories from the book, and the show, that I never thought were a national issue.

Cops always say one of two things when talking about the job. One, "It's a front row seat to the greatest show on Earth." Or two, "Welcome to the shit show." The unfortunate thing is, they are not just talking about what happens on the street.

Nick's newest book, The Dark Side of the Blue Line, illustrates yet another eyewitness account of what REALLY goes on inside the average sized, the metropolitan sized, the small town, and the largest police districts in the United States.

As a cop myself, when I am investigating a crime, and I talk to the two parties involved, I almost always say one thing, "There are three sides to every story, yours, theirs, and the truth." When it comes to law enforcement, the average citizen sees what they see personally, then they see what the department allows them to see, and that's it.

The things that Nick has covered over the years has been what is NOT typical for the public to see. It's from an insider's perspective. It's the truth.

As I said before, the delivery might not be for everyone, and some folks might take offense to it. The unfortunate thing is, sometimes the truth hurts, and in a world full of "Speak YOUR Truth," it's time to open your minds and eyes, and listen to the truth that Nick reveals.

Policing has always been a tough job, and it isn't getting any easier. There are pitfalls and peaks throughout any job that you pick, but very few of them can become detrimental to your mental health, or, ya know, murder you. That being said, police work has been very rewarding for many people, myself included.

If you want to experience what life is REALLY like, if you want to see how people REALLY treat other people, become a police officer. You'll thank yourself. There is no better life experience than 'the Job." We need more and more every year to sign up and "take the Oath." But, when the time comes, and you no longer feel like "You," and your old life is slipping away, grab hold of what's left and take inventory. Adapt and overcome only works for so long. Take heed to the warnings in this book, and others like it. The job will never love you as much as you love it. That's a fact. I want, as does Nick and every other cop out there, to see young cops

succeed and survive and thrive.

Nobody ever said life was going to be easy, but it shouldn't be made more difficult by those you work with. Enough of my rambling. I have my own demons to deal with. Now, go read about some of Nick's.

Logan Campbell

P.S.- Nick, shave your damn face, you look like a train-hopping hobo.

Table of contents

CHAPTER 1

RECRUITING

Let me start by saying that being a police officer is probably one of the most adventurous and satisfying jobs. Notice how I said job and not career? Starting a career in law enforcement now more than ever requires a "job" mentality for you to be able to survive the politics that come with it. This book will delve into what it really means to be an officer in the present day.

All of us have begun our careers by either being recruited or self-initiating an application into the job. If you were a thorough, type-A personality, then you went to the department you applied to and watched the high-speed, low-drag recruitment vids. You know, the videos that makes the department look like a mixture of *Lethal Weapon*, *Bad Boys*, and a little bit of *Free Willy* to calm the anti-police idiots down. It always starts with a SWAT member wearing a shirt that's two sizes too small and a mean mug. Eventually, it goes to K9 that highlights the dog that has the most bites or the dog that is so useless that they could afford to spare it for the day while Steven Spielberg films this shit show. The video will usually have music playing that gets you pumped up and excited about joining "a winning team." At the conclusion, if you're lucky, the chief or sheriff makes an appearance in a uniform riddled with metals and pins like a Cuban dictator. The chief or sheriff gives a compelling "we're family" monologue in the most robotic demeanor, all while not knowing what to do with their hands.

If you laughed while you read this, then you know it doesn't matter what department you work for; it's always the same recruitment mission. Now more than ever, it's all about just getting asses in seats for the academy. The problem with that is that is we are selling a fantasy and getting new officers or deputies with a false sense of what the job is or what it really means to be strapping on that uniform.

In an ideal world, a real recruitment video would go like this: a midnight officer in a cruiser, trying to stuff their face while filling out a report under a red light. Attending roll call and listening to countless commanders telling line officers how to do a job they haven't done in a long time, or who can't seal an envelope without an instruction manual. Then show how every traffic stop or subject stop turns into a justification why your enforcing law and order. Or show how after you spend countless hours investigating a case, collecting evidence, conducting follow up, and write a report worthy of a Pulitzer just to have the case executed by prosecutors that choose prosecution percentage over justice. Show a clip of a chief or sheriff's lack the core leadership skills or the integrity to weather "us" through this anti-cop climate.

I make light of recruitment videos, but they are often a factor in potential recruits deciding if they want to join an agency. In some cases, departments have faced litigation for recruitment videos and the false narrative they've created. They have also been used in civil cases when uses of force have occurred. Attorneys use recruitment videos to show that an agency is super aggressive or more into tactics than community policing.

When we look at recruitment, and hiring potential new officers or deputies, what are we doing to address the growing mental health crisis within law enforcement? Let's take that recruitment video and look at the money spent producing it. Now let's take a look at the operating budget for mental health programs for you and your co-workers. Crazy right? Mental health still continues to be something that's not addressed until it's too late, or stuffed away in the closet because leadership is afraid to deal with it.

 I'm not saying recruitment videos aren't necessary. We just need to be honest with our potential future officers or deputies. They need to understand that SWAT is not happening fresh off field training, and that K9 is not just about having a dog and taking home cruiser. Show the countless training hours it takes and physical fitness that's needed. Show the emergency visits to the vet because your K9 gets bored at home and eats weird shit, causing them to get sick. Or show the extreme scrutiny you're under after a bite, and how you need to be a legal expert to defend your actions to commanders who couldn't tell you case law nor have the balls to put on a bite suit.

I can't stress enough how, as a Sergeant, I watched recruits struggle when they got hired because they were sold a false narrative. Now, some were just not meant to do this job, and that should be sorted out in the hiring process and not in the academy or field training. These are people that grew up watching *LivePD* in between *Call of Duty* and *Sponge Bob*, and came up with an idea that being the police would be a great Facebook status. Or the TikTok cop that spends more time posting videos or selfies than handling calls for service. I'll talk about social media later in the book, but nothing frustrates me more than someone that gets hired because it looks cool and wants the social media exposure. Those officers, unfortunately, are the future of our profession if things don't change.

The second batch of officers I've watched struggle are the ones sold the *Die Hard* movie profession but instead got the three-ring circus. These officers get hired and get drilled in from day one: "Family first, family first, family first," and then when they finish the academy, they realize that it's "staffing first, and your family can wait." They discover that law enforcement is like a cult, in the sense that we are very guarded with what's behind the curtains, and as long as you don't rock the boat, things will be peachy. New officers discover that your body will go through some extreme changes from weight gain or loss to sleep deprivation. They learn that the moment you walk across that stage and except that badge, things will change outside of work. Family dynamics will change and have to adapt to your schedule, moods, and anti-social behavior. If you're single, the likelihood of finding a partner outside of the law enforcement or first responder pool is very low. If you're married, the likelihood that you'll be divorced or commit adultery is extremely high. I got your attention on that one, but it's the dirty truth.

One thing we have to prepare our prospective hires for is that they relinquish their first amendment right. The days of taking to social media or publicly speaking your mind is over. Writing this part of the book, I just Googled "officer fired for social media post" and the results speak for themselves. I will get into that further later in the book, but it's a topic that needs to be addressed during the recruitment. Your new social media is the coffee huddle at 2am in a back ally or car to car. Even with body cameras you're limited on your right to speak freely. For some that doesn't sit well, but it is a reality. Don't get me wrong, if you're going on social media posting racist or homophobic shit, then you're an idiot and shouldn't be wearing a uniform.

Another topic that needs to be addressed is financial responsibility. Cops are the worst at saving money, and exceptionally good at blowing it on stupid shit. We will work a million hours of overtime for a gun, a trip to the Caribbean, or clothes, but saving for retirement? Good luck. I am just as guilty of this as the next person, and lived my law enforcement career paycheck to paycheck. It wasn't until I left the profession and started counseling that I discovered why we do that. Our profession is day to day, I'd even say hour to hour. We have no idea what that next traffic stop will bring or if that domestic call will result in our last. We spend our money and live in the moment subconsciously. Now, had I of known that early on in my career, I would have still pissed away my money, just less of it.

Speaking about fiscal responsibility is something we really don't do but personal finance is one of the leading causes of suicides in law enforcement. Imagine if we addressed it during annual reviews. Relax, I'm not talking about running credit reports and starting an investigation into your finances. I'm talking about departments investing in financial planners to help keep officers and deputies from falling into financial pits.

Recruitment has to be a secondary priority in building a "new" law enforcement profession. Yes, I said second. Leadership is priority number one right now in our failing profession.

CHAPTER 2

LEADERSHIP

I could write a whole book just on this topic. As a matter of fact, my first book "Police Mental Barricade: A survivor's guide to poor law enforcement leadership," speaks extensively about police leadership and the lack of it. I was surprised at how that book has resonated with officers, deputies, and particularly in the military. The lack of leadership or the type of toxic leadership that prevails is across the board and doesn't care what uniform you wear.

One of the things crushing morale and killing this profession is leadership. The war on police is not just from the public but internally. You are more likely to get fucked by your agency than by the public you serve. My wife, who was a deputy at the Alexandria City Virginia Adult Detention Center, would come home after working 12 hours on midnights and say, "I'm more afraid of the leadership than the inmates." She would tell me about people in "leadership" positions making decisions that made no sense, and if officers challenged them, they were punished by being placed in housing units that required extra work and excessive personal protection gear during COVID. My wife was routinely punished for being an independent thinker or for challenging the commander in charge of COVID response.

As a former Sergeant this infuriated me, but I was powerless to help. I watched her mental health deteriorate due to lack of sleep, feeling demoralized, and at times panic attacks on her way to work. When she asked for help, she was put through shit and labeled as "crazy." When she put in her notice to leave the department due to mental health issues, the department's response was to tell her that she owed them $20,000 for the cost of the academy and training. I don't tell you this to trash the department, but to give you an example of how good leadership can help prevent a mental health crisis by treating employees with compassion and dignity.

COVID exposed a lot of poor leaders and made way for administrative warriors. For the past 20 years in law enforcement, we've been in peace time relatively. After Ferguson and the death of George Floyd, law enforcement was thrown into war time. Before I get emails about the term "war time," relax, Karens. I'm referring to rough seas in the profession, a time when you need someone leading from the front and being hit with the same bottles and soaked with the same piss balloons. Someone that understands that just because a complaint comes in, doesn't mean that you're the next Officer Chauvet.

I watched in my old department as keyboard warriors destroyed morale while advancing their careers. This is always the problem when poor leaders are about to get exposed. They resort to deflecting off of their own inability to lead by singling out people that are a threat. I watched as good officers were targeted and careers destroyed because of retaliation.

In one instance, an officer came forward while going through a divorce and advised Internal Investigations of wrong doing. Granted this wrong doing was actionable and definitely required punishment. What it didn't require was for his career to be destroyed and for him to be lied to.

He was initially told by the Chief of Police that his punishment would be 30 days suspended no pay. It was totally warranted, and being a good officer with integrity, he accepted his punishment. Several hours later, he received a phone call from Internal Investigations saying that he was being terminated. Confused, this officer attempted to get ahold of the Chief but was unsuccessful. Later, he found out that the Chief reversed his decision, and instead of facing the officer, he took the coward's way out.

I can tell you countless stories of this Chief destroying peoples' careers and being dishonest. It shows that a person's resume and accomplishments doesn't make them a great leader. In our profession, we rely heavily on certificates and certifications but care little about results. I've taken a shit ton of leadership courses, and the biggest take away from all the certificates sitting in a box is get breakfast before class and don't sit in the back. In full transparency, when I was trying to get promoted, I signed up for every leadership course. I spent more time in class being slowly killed by PowerPoint presentations than actually being shown what makes a good leader. Every course was about holding people accountable, documentation, and discipline. Then I got promoted and realized that I couldn't be that kind of leader. I quickly understood that my job was to be a mentor and to guide people. This didn't sit well with upper command.

On several occasions, I was orally counseled for being too pro-officer or "covering for my people." This cost me assignments to specialized units while I watched people that destroyed morale and kissed ass advance. Our profession is better than that and this is why it is a mess right now. We have dinosaurs leading departments and making policy in the comfort of their office or "teleworking," while the people with boots on the ground are

Leadership or lack of it is why we have protestors destroying entire cities. Stand down orders while small businesses are fire bombed and politicians use it as a backdrop or platform. The word "reform" has a dirty taste from being crammed down our throats. As media outlets disparage our integrity and blame line officers for law enforcement policy, we have chiefs and sheriffs taking a knee to appease criminals. We have municipalities creating murals for criminals while fallen officers can't even get a plaque for the ultimate sacrifice. We watch as "defund the police" trends on social media and our leadership stands idly by as pensions and benefits are reduced and then scratch their heads wondering why recruitment is down or why seasoned officers are walking away from the job.

The very survival of our profession hinges on immediate change in leadership across the country. Soon, case law allowing us to keep citizens safe will be challenged and with no clear leadership from our profession opposing it. If anything, current leadership will embrace it in an effort to score points with radical groups and secure political backing for funds. This causes a ripple effect that ultimately negatively impacts the line officers. Uses of forces will be turned over to civilians and punishment dished out inconsistently and at the sway of the political climate. Poor leaders embrace this way of policing because it allows for plausible deniability with the troops, the "it's not me fucking you, it's the civilian complaint review board." This also benefits municipalities because it takes liability away from them and shifts it onto the civilian review.

 Leadership knows this is coming. They know it because they are already placating radical groups with seats at the policy table. Don't get me wrong, good, law-abiding citizens have every right to demand excellence from law enforcement. What shouldn't happen—and is upon us— is criminals having the authority to make policy. Right now, we have criminals saying, "I don't like that you keep arresting me for doing drugs, so from now on doing drug enforcement is a no no." Never in my life or when I started in law enforcement would I believe that shit would become a reality. You have municipalities saying hard narcotics are legal now and that this is a good thing because we spend money fighting the war on drugs. And the best part is citizens eat that ship up and say, "That makes sense." Meanwhile, when they come home and the door is kicked in and shit is stolen they ask, "What are the police doing to prevent this?" Then we have a chief or sheriff say publicly, "We'll do better." No motherfucker, speak up and tell the public why crime is out of control.

Our leadership has caused this climate of hatred towards law enforcement by not embracing change and allowing line officer to be part of the policy decision-making process. They've chased off great future leaders by crushing morale and deterring forward thinking. The ones that stay (like us) are committed and have the belief that everything will get better and that change is on the way. But in reality, our profession is so infiltrated with positional equity leaders and politicians wearing a uniform.

I'd like to imagine our future leaders in our profession being vetted by the rank and file. No, not the rank and file doing the hiring for Chief, but the rank and file having a seat at the table with officials in charge of making the hiring decisions. A seasoned street cop can smell bullshit from a mile away. I remember in my old agency when we did a national search for our Chief, the city held a town hall meeting at our headquarters. In this room were the entire staff for the police department (roughly 200). In walks this guy, small in stature, who looked like time beat the shit out of him hard. He used a very low and soft voice, which later I learned was a tactic of his to keep you engaged because you focus on trying to understand the asshole. He starts talking to the room about how our agency is damaged and people have been scared and that scars need time to heal. Yeah, I know… you already get the picture of where this is going. This guy came from a large department in California where he was shrouded in controversy, and ultimately forced out. He addressed it because everyone was thinking about it. Basically, he used the department's disfunction against them by claiming he was a victim of a political hit job which was total bullshit, but we didn't know that until about a year later.

As this guy was talking, I could feel a pit in my stomach growing. Change is hard for cops and we know that, but this was something different. It was the sense that something was wrong with this guy and that in some way it would be my problem. Unfortunately, I was proven right just three years later. Don't worry we'll get to that. My point is that if you do this job long enough, developing the skill of detecting bullshit is a given. We know when we are about to get bent over and when to prepare for a shit storm.

I speak about the Chief of Police position a lot on my podcast "The Roll Call Room Podcast" and get a lot of emails about it. When I was interviewing Lieutenant Colonel Grossman (author of "On Killing," "Killology," and "On Combat") we talked about how the Chief position has swung to a political appointment and in actuality no longer a law-enforcement position. Chiefs are more concerned about staying in good favor of the mayor or city manager than doing the job they were sworn in for. Most good chiefs will only last three to four years because of political change or forced out by politicians for doing the right thing in the wrong way politically. The remedy to this is to abolish the Chief of Police position across the country.

Hear me out. Departments should adapt a sheriff structure where the head of the department is voted in. This person obviously needs law enforcement experience and whatever prettily framed certificate that you wish, but must campaign to the people for the position. This person will be held to the standard of his or her campaign platform. The position is a three-year cycle and unions have the ability to campaign for change if the person is a disaster. I know what you're thinking, "Well, then we'll get a political hack." That's a risk you'll run, but you're almost guaranteed a political hack with a chief. Someone who sways by political pressure and has no core standard. With the sheriff structure, the transparency within the department is greater. The risk of scandal being covered up and then leaked during a campaign tends to keep sheriffs semi-honest. I've seen things within my old department swept under the rug and never spoken about, all in the interest of protecting the Chief of Police.

This strategy isn't foolproof or guaranteed to solve the leadership problem, but it definitely makes departments more accountable and allows for the type of reform *we* need, rather than the reform radicals are calling for.

CHAPTER 3

SOCIAL MEDIA

Oh social media... I honestly think that when some social media platforms were created, it all but solidified the loss of law enforcement jobs because of stupidity. Don't get me wrong, I'm a big supporter of social media being used in law enforcement on so many levels. Where we as a profession went wrong was not embracing it early on or even now.

Social media for officers, or your right to exercise the first amendment, is currently a hot topic. Departments have fired people for posting personal opinions or posting negative things about their departments. In some cases it is warranted, but in most, it really isn't. Instead, it's a tactic used to censor officers or control any negativite sentiments about the agency.

When I was forced out of my agency, one of the outlets I used to vent my frustration and expose the Alexandria City Police Department was Facebook. Being a newly "former" member of the department, they had no control of what I posted nor could anyone refute what I said because the social media general orders forbid it. What happened when I started using my podcast and social media to share my experience surprised even me. When I released my first book, I was really in for a shock. Commanders, people in the upper tier of the department, created fake Facebook accounts in an attempt to attack me personally. Detectives within the department created photoshopped pictures of me and called me a liar and a thief. When that didn't silence me— and I used it to gain more listeners—they saw it was garnering support for me, they switched to invading Facebook Live's and using fake screen names like "Nick Steals" or "Ruggiero Nicksteals."

In one instance, a commander who was too stupid not to use his home IP address attempted to harass my daughter by telling her vile things about me.

When I attempted to report this activity to the City of Alexandria, including the mayor and city council, I was told to fuck off. I filed ethics complaints and was told no wrong doing had been committed.

There was zero accountability, and what made it worse was some of the officer and detectives engaged in this behavior were people I had considered friends. Some were people I'd supervised and prevented from getting fired. Others were the worst cops but I had protected them.

Social media in this instance was used as a weapon by multiple people in an attempt to silence me. It is used like this a lot to bully fellow officers. When I was going through that daily harassment, all I could think of was how thin the blue line really is. People I respected and thought highly of creating fake accounts to attack me and my family blew my mind, but later understood that it was because I was speaking negatively about the department and for people that are brainwashed by the toxicity that scared them.

Social media has the ability within law enforcement to take our profession into the type of reform needed. The officer who has an Instagram account doing physical fitness videos and motivating other cops to stay fit and help with mental health shouldn't be crushed by the department for having social media. I've seen this time and time again where morale is crushed because an officer is reprimanded for having videos of himself doing workouts, but a TikTok of another officer dancing around like a jackass in the public is praised. The moral compass of some of these decision makers is astounding.

We've created a culture within our profession to fear social media and to "be careful" while having a social media account. Yes, there's a reason why we have these policies and it generally is because someone has fucked up. In the instances where you're on social media posting racist or political opinions that clearly impact law enforcement negatively, you should be reprimanded. The disciplinary measures should be fair and consistent.

In my old department, an officer James who was gay decided to get wear his dress uniform to get married. Like every wedding, he and his husband took pictures in uniform. A commander who clearly had an issue with this officer's lifestyle printed off the picture and documented the officer for not having the chief's approval prior to posting a picture in uniform. This then turned into combing through his Facebook account and documenting him for each incident where he wore his uniform without approval.

Fast forward a few years, this officer came to eventually work for me. While looking through his squad file (which was two inches thick), I came across him being documented for things that every officer does on a routine basis. It was all clearly retaliation and painted a picture of this commander being biased.

This type of social media enforcement had an extreme adverse effect on that officer. The mental health issues this created was preventable. They weighed on the officer and prevented promotions and assignments to specialized units. The officer was blacklisted within the department and it allowed him to be targeted from every positional equity leader.

Further in his career, James came to work for a new sergeant. This sergeant was very insecure about his abilities to supervise and extremely politically vocal on Facebook. So vocal that it was well known within the department that this sergeant was considered an extremist in his political views. He had things that were posted on Facebook that were not becoming of an officer and violated the departments social media general orders.

This sergeant was not investigated or documented for social media general orders violations, but rather elevated within the department. Ultimately, this sergeant participated in getting James terminated.

Actions like this infuriate me and frustrate good cops. The inconsistency of dishing out punishment is something I talk about a lot in my first book. It's a "who you know" sort of profession. Everyone doesn't get treated the same and rules only apply to certain people. We'll address that more in depth later.

Social media is not the boogie man. Utilized correctly it can actually counter the radical movement of "defund the police" and other groups that are clueless about how law enforcement works.

Even to this day, leaders within law enforcement treat Facebook, Instagram, and Twitter like the plague. Mostly because they don't understand it or just see the negative shit people post, such as negative police interactions. They look at social media as a nuisance and not something they can use to directly relate to the public, staff, or drive a narrative at an active scene.

Then you have leaders who listen to Public Information Officers (PIO's) who say that social media is only good for dancing around like a circus animal to get 100 likes. They utilize social media for press releases or traffic updates. So the public sees the departments social media account as a stiff authoritative outlet. This is the pitfall a lot of agencies run into.

Take a moment right now and look at your agency's social media accounts. I would venture to say that it resembles this: K9 pictures, incident updates, academy graduation pictures, and some funny videos or pictures for "National Donut Day." This is fine and it's a safe page according to a lot of law enforcement agency leaders. What they aren't understanding is that 50% of their recruitment issue can be solved just by revamping their social media presence. Because it's an applicant's market right now, social media is the best way to check out your potential new agency. A lot of millennials are attracted to social media and check out what type of environment they'd be working in. Applicants are more likely to apply for an agency where the social media is informative, interactive, and forward-thinking.

One thing we don't see utilized by agencies is Facebook Live or Instagram Live. This is an incredibly powerful tool to use for law enforcement. This gives the agency the ability to drive a narrative rather than respond to it.

Utilizing a live platform should be available to selected line officers. If you're a commander reading this, relax. Notice how I said, "selected." This would actually require agencies to send people to social media and public information training. Training that teaches you how to not look like Ricky Bobby on camera and not look robotic. A lot of agencies have officers that are really good at public speaking and can be great representatives for an agency.

It takes two seconds at a major crime scene to click that little "Live" button and give viewers a rundown of what is going on. This sets the narrative tone for what's happening, and forces the biased media to chase "our" narrative which is the truth. This is a tactic that dramatically reduces the ability for social media master's degree recipients to spin the truth.

Too many times, our profession shy away from making a comment or utilizing social media to get the first word in. Our favorite statement is "No comment." This has allowed the media to make up stories and crucify good police officers during justified shootings.

For years, social media has been used as a weapon against law enforcement. Careers have been ended because of it. But investigations have also been solved. Yet law enforcement lacks the skill or ingenuity to harness it for our benefit.

CHAPTER 4

FALSE REPORTING

OF CRIME

This is a chapter that my fellow law enforcement colleagues will understand and my non-law enforcement readers will get infuriated over. The intention of this chapter is to shed light onto and make law enforcement agencies more transparent when reporting crime to the public.

Since the early days of police work, crime statistics have been an instrumental part of fighting crime. In one form or another, crime reporting affects every aspect of the way the public functions. If crime reporting is high in one area, then the housing market takes a dive or businesses are reluctant to open.

High crime reporting effects budgeting for municipalities. More resources are allocated to "high crime" areas to reduce crime and improve quality of life.

Schools are affected by crime reporting as well. Grants are awarded to schools in higher crime areas to give children in these communities better opportunities. Programs like "No Children Left Behind" were birthed in part because of high crime reporting.

High crime reporting helps politicians secure elections and Commonwealth Attorneys or District Attorneys "take a hard stance on crime." The judicial system benefits the most from "high crime." More judges are added to preside over cases, more funds are allocated to public defenders, and more jobs are created for probation and parole.

The interesting thing about all of this is how manipulating crime statistics can sway crime reports. This happens all the time, and it's happening right now all over the country.

In my old department, I watched it happen a lot. Each week, our crime analyst would email the department our crime statistics. Each report was broken down into Part 1 crime: robbery, rape, homicide, violent offenses, and grand larcenies. Part 2 crime or nuisance crimes: alcohol offenses, drugs, drinking while driving, and destructions. Our job as Sergeants within the police department's patrol division was to supervise the line officers. The grunts on the streets. They would receive a call for service, gather the facts, and be required to write a report. The report title or offense is how those crime report's statistics are affected. After sending in the report, sergeants are required to read the reports and suggest edits if needed. After review, these reports are approved and sent electronically to our records department. Once they are transmitted, the offense is locked in and that triggers the crime report statistics to either go up or down.

Command staff and the Chief of Police would have monthly meetings called Strategic Response Strategies (SRS). In these meetings, each sector Captain would have to explain to command staff and the Chief why specific Part 1 or Part 2 crimes were high or how they will reduce them. A lot of times, these meetings turned into a circle jerk called, "look what I'm doing" and "look how I got my numbers down."

After these meetings, commanders would give orders for crime to be under reported or under cut. How could this happen? Well, it's actually really easy and done across the country at a lot of agencies. If you respond to an assault that involves a minor injury, you classify it as "assault and battery" rather than "felony assault and battery." Instead of reporting a robbery, you classify it as "larceny from person." Homicides are classified as "sudden death" so that our department could choose when to classify something as a homicide and keep statistics low.

As the Sergeant of the Community Policing Unit, I saw a lot of crime report manipulation. Our unit was very proactive. Our job was to go into "high crime" areas and do proactive policing. This included making arrests for alcohol offenses, drug offenses, and weapon violations. This produced a lot of arrests and caused nuisance crimes to skyrocket.

On a routine basis, I was ordered to "cool off" the enforcement because the crime stats were too high for the quarter. The first time I was told this, my heart sank. I remember going home and talking to my wife about it. I felt like it was a betrayal to my officers, and more importantly the public. I was being asked to allow crime to happen because if we didn't go looking for it, it didn't exist.

This happened all the time, and still continues to happen. The reason it happens is because the general public doesn't know how to decipher crime statistics. Recently, my old department posted a 19% increase in Part 1 crime but a 52% reduction in nuisance crimes. The general public celebrated the 52% reduction in nuisance crime and completely ignored the 19% increase in Part 1 crime. This no fault of theirs because law enforcement makes it a point not to educate them on the difference.

This is one of the darkest parts of law enforcement, one that's been going on for a long time. The ability to manipulate crime statistics is extremely powerful and has the ability to impact so many things.

The ability to manipulate crime report statistics has to be monitored and regulated by the FBI which is where all local agencies report crime statistics to. Agencies need to be held accountable for manipulating these crime statistics including loss of federal grants and loss of accreditation.

Officer's should have the ability to anonymously report supervisors, command staff, and/or the chief of police to the justice department for ordering crimes to be reclassified to manipulate crime statistics.

No one should manipulate crime statistics in order to effect funding, budgeting, or any other financial gain. Departments will hang an officer out to dry for lying or being untruthful but on the top floor in conference rooms they are doing far worse and what makes it worse is its a deception to the citizens. We are lying to the public and smiling while doing it. This is not the oath that we took and its an embarrassment to our profession.

CHAPTER 5

COMMUNITY

POLICING FALSEHOOD

I've spent almost my entire law enforcement career working in community policing. I've devoted countless hours to working in the community and "mingling" with citizens and gaining trust. I was the poster child for community policing. I supervised 12 highly motivated officers in the community policing unit. I reminded them on a daily basis that community policing was not just a philosophy, but a necessity in police work. When commanders and other sergeants made fun of the community policing unit, I came to its defense. In one instance in my former agency, a fellow sergeant took pictures of my officers and superimposed things onto them to make fun of the community policing events we did.

During the holidays, I spearheaded food collections for people in the community and organized a community Thanksgiving dinner for 100 people in the community.

During Christmas, my team collected over 3000 toys and put on 18 holidays events to disperse toys to under privileged kids.

When my team wasn't burning the candle at both ends during the holidays, they were ridiculed and labeled the "hug a thug program" or the "BBQ squad."

I watched as these holiday events were used as positional equity by commanders and the Chief of Police to gain the community's trust, but in reality they didn't care about what we were doing.

I list some of the events, not to brag about them or to impress you, but to give validity to my findings.

These findings are that community policing philosophy is bullshit. It's bullshit because of the lack of *community* in community policing. In law enforcement, community policing is used as a con or a bait-and-switch. We go into these communities and we do a little song and dance in hopes that the public buys the bullshit. We drill into our new officers that community policing is important and the backbone of the agency, but in reality, it's a bail out. When shit goes sideways in another state, or some idiot in our profession fucks up, we withdraw some currency from the social bank. I've seen it time and time again where we think dancing like a king's jester equates to community policing. Or doing these music videos where we get together and act like the village people is the same as engaging within the community.

Community policing and community engagement are two completely different things. Community engagement is recognizing that the policing department needs to mirror the community.

Having tattoo policing and beard policy in your agency is an example of this. Do you think that Sally what's-her-name gives two shits that you have a sleeve of tattoos while someone is breaking into her house? No! Departments are more focused on these policies than actually doing community engagement.

I was always amazed when law enforcement command staff worried about the demographics of an agency mirroring the community, but not concerned that the public can care two fucks what your racial make-up is versus having officers look like human beings and not fresh off an Abercrombie and Fitch ad.

Community policing has been destroyed by law enforcement leadership using and wheeling it around as a get out of jail free card. Whenever they get called out for racial inequality, they immediately start rattling off community policing initiatives, but can't tell you how those initiatives were started or who started them.

In my old department, the chief would use the community policing unit as a wild card. Anytime he was about to face opposition or be hit with budget concerns, the community policing unit was deployed into the community so that the local press could take pictures. It would make me sick to see commanders show up in their shinny shoes and clean pressed uniforms to take pictures and then take off. Many times, officers that worked for me would feel discouraged because they can see these commanders using us for their own benefit.

The term "community policing" should be abolished. It's a catchphrase at this point and is honestly disingenuous. The truth is community policing stopped being effective long ago, but it's catchy and looks good on t-shirts so it's still around.

The true name for community policing in law enforcement is being a good cop. Knowing your community and having your finger on the pulse. If you're a good street cop and you know your shit, then community policing doesn't need a title but rather support from the command staff.

I don't want the takeaway from this chapter to be "fuck community policing." I want you to understand, from someone that lived and swore by it, that it's not the only way in policing to form a partnership with the community. It's time for the next generation of law enforcement to create a new culture that embraces and supports its community.

CHAPTER 6

BULLY MENTALITY

When I started in law enforcement it was like a family, and in any family .you have disagreements. I always believed in the thin blue line and how it was the line between order and chaos.

As I continued in law enforcement, I discovered that there are some within our profession that are evil and enjoy creating misery. Everyone has them in their agency. The crew of people who are stuck in high school and enjoy being part of the popular group: that group of people that dictate what happens because command staff is too afraid of them to performance manage them.

In my old agency, we had a faction of officers that created a bully culture. A culture that eroded into promotional processes and assignments into specialized units. There was a female commander in particular that gossiped and enjoyed spreading rumors and watching drama unfold.

I routinely watched as this faction of officers were given special treatment because they were considered the "cool kids." When I got promoted to Sergeant, I had to manage one of these officers and it was a nightmare. This officer was a loud mouth and bullied other officers on a routine basis. I would keep newer officers away from this officer to avoid them being poisoned by the toxicity.

Bullying in our profession happens every day. It happens between co-workers and it happens from our command staff. We are a profession that eats its own for no reason. We talk about the thin blue line, but over the years we've lost what that means. The thin blue line only applies when an officer is killed in the line of duty or when its National Police Week.

I see on social media officers post about the anti-police movement and the radicals looking to defund the police. In actuality, the problem isn't the outside element trying to destroy us, it's internal. We are rotting from the inside by ruthless cowards that claim to be part of the thin blue line but will cut your throat to get a little bit ahead. These are the same people that create an "us" versus "them" mentality, and if you don't follow their ideology then you're not considered part of the team.

We have a major problem that must first be solved from within before we can defend ourselves from the radical faction of people that are set on disrupting our mission

and oath. Here are examples… First one is a Lieutenant
now…

CHAPTER 7

RELATIONSHIPS

Let me start by saying I'm no relationship expert. Actually far from it. I don't have a fancy degree in a mahogany frame; I didn't go to college for 12 years to study different theories on how and why relationships end. What I do have is 25 years with the same woman that started before my law enforcement career.

I tell you this because the things that I've done to this woman over the past five years are terrible, and in all honesty, enough to make anyone walk away. When I met my wife, we were in our teens and just starting out in life. We got married young and started out in New York City trying to make ends meet. I'd always wanted to be in law enforcement from the time I was five. My wife knew it was my ambition and my purpose in life. She fell in love with a kid who laughed a lot and always saw the good in people. A person who always enjoyed life and did spontaneous things to feel fulfilled.

When the opportunity came to work in Virginia and start a new life there, she didn't hesitate to pack up our kids and move. She altered her life for my ambition of being in law enforcement.

During the police academy, she stood by while I destroyed my body and started to shift away from the man she fell in love with. Early on in training, the instructors drilled into us that we needed to get out of the civilian mentality and start thinking like cops.

I stopped being friends with people outside of law enforcement and pressured my wife to do the same. She was a cop's wife now and needed to play the part. When I started field training and started working nights, she needed to go to sleep alone and wake up to an empty bed. I remember her trying to stay up as late as she could "just in case."

On mornings when I should have been home, she would wake up and franticly text or call asking, "Where are you?" She became well-educated in legal words and terms like "Booking, DWI, and PBT."

My wife had to keep the kids quiet so I could sleep four hours and go back on shift. She took the brunt of my attitude when I woke up tired and couldn't take it out on anyone else. When she would tell me "I love you" before leaving for my shift, I would get angry for no reason because I felt like she was guilting me not to go into work.

On days off when she wanted to go out or do things with the kids, I would retreat onto the couch and stare at the TV like a zombie or watch COPS. Stories at the dinner table were about crime scenes and the horrible things I'd seen.

When "friends" from the department would come over for a BBQ or we would go out, she would sit there and listen to us tell war stories and relive graphic scenes. I'd look over and see her interest slowly drift away but still hang in there because it was important to me. To repay her for her commitment, I'd work overtime on special days like anniversaries and holidays. I'd tell her it was for the money, but in reality it was self-gratification because the job was like a drug. I constantly needed the adrenaline rush—the high of feeling in control and living dangerously.

As time went on working in law enforcement I put in more time and commitment to my agency because that's what gets you promoted. On days off I would study for promotional processes, and when she would tell me to take a break I'd take it as disloyalty instead of a caring, devoted wife worried about her husband.

When promotional processes were over, she would sit and listen to me talk on the phone for hours with other promotional candidates dissecting the process and making each other feel good, but I wouldn't sit on the phone with my wife for five minutes to talk about how I'm doing or how the kids were.

Then when I got promoted and was excited to throw myself at the agency more and change my entire family dynamics and schedule, my wife would sit and encourage me, all while knowing that she'd have to sacrifice more time away from me and I'd be away from the kids even more.

My wife would get dragged to community events and have to watch as the department used and abused me while dangling another carrot in my face for another promotion. She'd listen to me go on for hours about how unfair and incompetent command staff was and how they didn;t appreciate my sacrifices.

While climbing the ladder and "making a name for myself," she watched as I lived two lives. One life that promised great things but required 110% of me, and another life with responsibility and structure. In my head, all the time justifying the means in the end would make everything worth it.

During the end of my career, my wife watched as I kept making excuses for cowardly leaders and my "friends" that would stab me in the back again and again. We would get into fights where I argued to her that they wouldn't betray me because were a brotherhood and a family. There was no way they would accuse me of being a thief because of a podcast and because I took the lieutenant process as a patrol officer. She warned me not to rock the boat and to stop testing the command staff's limit.

As a repayment for all of her commitment and loyalty, I betrayed her trust and destroyed my family. When my department was doing everything in its power to get rid of me, I entered the most self-destructive part of my life. I was doing things intentionally to get her to leave me and run away. I'd goad her into arguments and push her to pack up the kids and leave me alone. She would cry

herself to sleep at night and I would roll over and ignore

her. I became the worst version of myself, but I didn't

care. I lied to get out of the previous lie, and when that

didn't work, I made up lavished stories to cover up my

wrongs.

All through this, she wouldn't leave. At one point, after

the department threw me out like trash and destroyed me

mentally and emotionally, I ran away from home. I went

online and booked a trip and ran away with the intention

of never returning again. My kids hated me before I left

and my wife wanted someone that I wasn't anymore. My

life at that moment was over, and I was angry and

disappointed with myself. I hated who I was and how I'd

just given up.

While I was down, certain commanders and people within the Alexandria City Police Department created the fake Facebook accounts to attack me personally, calling me a thief and a liar. While I was down, one person took it upon themselves to contact my wife and share with her some of my ugly secrets. Things she suspected and feared were corroborated by this person, and that destroyed her.

While I was battling this inner-conflict, my wife was working for the City of Alexandria's sheriff's department as a deputy in the jail. I was now compromising her physical safety with my recklessness and disregard for our marriage. People that hated me in her command took it out on her nightly by assigning her to dangerous housing units.

I was running a podcast on law enforcement mental health and putting out my first book discussing mental health, but didn't see right in front of me that the woman I married was falling apart. When she would leave for work, she would sit in her car and sob and not want to go because she was fraying at the seams. This still wasn't enough for me to wake up and change; instead I continued to be destructive.

When all the cards were on the table and she was walking out the door, I pushed her even further because I felt like a failure. I felt like the only value I had was being a cop and that was gone. I treated my old department and the job like a relationship, but in reality it was a one-sided love. The relationship I should have been focusing on all along was the one with my wife. I had led a double life for so long that I'd forgotten what it was like to be in a marriage.

The hardest part was finally being vulnerable with her and saying, "I'm sorry I hurt you, please forgive me."

Too many times we give everything we have to our profession and our agency and forget that the most important relationships are the ones that don't require a uniform. The ones we love are on the ride along, but don't have to be part of the trauma.

After all of this, I still continue to struggle in trying to be the best husband I can. I have days where the depression of losing my law enforcement career makes me sick. I sometimes have days where the weight of what I've done to my wife, and the collateral damage I created, makes me feel sick to my stomach. I struggle with knowing what type of husband I should be, since I've been broken for so long. I struggle with telling my wife the truth because lying was just easier.

All of these struggles are now worth more than pretending to be something I wasn't or the man that I couldn't even recognize anymore. I can at least look at myself in the mirror for the first time in a long time.

CHAPTER 8

RAZOR-THIN BLUE

LINE

The sooner you realize that the thin blue line is razor thin, the better it will be for your career and your mental health. You can wear the cop t-shirts and represent every cop company by slapping their logo on your duty bag all day long, but the reality of it is that our thin blue line is getting thinner by the year.

When I joined law enforcement, it was a brotherhood and no one ever crossed the thin blue line. Fast-forward to the current climate and we can't determine who our friends are anymore. This is becoming an issue across the country, and not just among command staff. We have rookies expecting to become sergeants in two years, and with a sense of entitlement the moment they sign the offer letter. The worst part is that we humor it, because we have a national staffing issue since no one wants to be the police.

I learned the hard way about how thin the blue line is when I left the Alexandria City Police Department. It wasn't enough that they succeeded in destroying my career and my personal life, but the department that I spent years dedicating my time and energy into decided to make sure I couldn't get hired anywhere else.

When I was forced out of my agency, I had no contingency plan. I never prepared for how vile and vindictive my old agency and some bad apples would be in their plan to prevent me from ever working in law enforcement again. It was the first time I realized how very thin the blue line is.

When I was unemployed, and very close to losing my house and car, it was the help of kind strangers from my podcast that made me realize that the blue line was dead all together.

One of the fans of my podcast Tim Allen (no not *that* Tim Allen) took it upon himself to take up a collection. He didn't know it, but that was how I was able to survive for a bit. He is the reason why the thin blue line survives for me, and he understands the meaning of friendship and family.

I learned also that it didn't matter how many people I helped get ahead or promoted on the job. The moment you walk out of your headquarters, that loyalty is over. Retirees see that a lot. They retire and slowly people disappear or stop contacting you.

When I did hear from anyone from my old department, it was to feed me information about the chief or ask for me to file a Freedom of Information Act request.

I watched as "friends" on Facebook dwindled and the gossiping started. The worst part was watching people whose weddings and births of their children I'd attended talk ill of me or contribute to the bullying.

One of my friends, and also someone I supervised, started to come to my coffee shop when he was put on administrative leave pending the outcome of an internal investigation. It was good therapy for me to witness from the outside what the department was putting him through. He and I would have conversations about the legality of what the department was doing and how vicious our co-workers were. I also got to witness that mentality I like to call "the gambler." Like a gambler on a hot streak, you don't want to walk away from the table. You're a little down but you know it'll level out or be back in the plus column soon.

I listened to him justify why the same sergeant in Internal Investigations (IA) asked this question and say that thing, all while trying to make you feel like everything will work out and before you know it you'll be back to work.

When the day came for him to meet with the chief, I warned him to be cautious and not set his expectations high. He was optimistic and eager to just get it over with. What he didn't expect was for the chief to give him a 30-day suspension only to have IA call him hours later to say he was terminated.

The devastation that he felt and the depression was something I could relate to. I held my "I told you so" for another day, and did what a family does. I shut up and sat and listened to him vent. I gave him advice on what not to do and on what his options were. His main concern was his family and supporting them while he picked up the pieces. I offered him a safety net and a job for the time being. while he figured out the next step.

Watching his friends from the department's motor unit—which is a very close group of officers—retreat from him was, in a way, comforting for me. Don't get me wrong, it's horrible but I realized it wasn't me and my situation that made these people betray me and do what they did. It's our culture. It's ingrained in us from the day we get all dressed up and go to day one of the academy. "Us" versus "them," and if you're not us then you're them. If you're a cop in trouble... stand back, because it's like wearing an explosive vest.

We will run into gun fire or go balls to the wall for people we don't even know, just because they called 911. But if an officer needs emotional or mental help? Forget it. That blue line gets real fuzzy when you get accused of something or you speak against your agency. Instead of embracing constructive criticism, or realizing that the agency isn't always right, the reaction is to distance yourself as far as you can.

Months after his departure, this officer and I were outside my cafe smoking a cigar and drinking coffee and I asked him, "Five years ago, would you ever think the two of us would be here with each other?" His response shocked me a bit because he said, "Yes, because you always cared and never took sides when it was the popular thing to do. I didn't understand what you went through, and honestly thought you were a bit crazy, but now that I've gone through it and lived to see the other side, I get it. It was just a job and they were just people in the job."

I agree partially. It *is* just a job and I agree that these people are just people in it, but I also know that it doesn't have to be this way. We've come so far in law enforcement with training and tactics, but we continue to lose more officers to suicide then we do to line of duty deaths. Why? Because we haven't learned from our mistakes and continue to keep bullies in our profession that erase the blue line with the slippery tails behind them and the tears of family members of people they've destroyed to get ahead. A line that's supposed to be tied together with strength, honor, integrity, and good intentions severed by bad intentions and hate.

CHAPTER 9

MENTAL HEALTH

I will shout at the top of my lungs until my last breath about mental health awareness in the first responder community (including 911 dispatchers).

I've traveled all over doing speaking engagements thanks to my first book, and I always say the same thing to the audience, "Who is responsible for the mental health program in your agency?" Typically, the answer I get is, "Human Resources." BULLSHIT! It's you!

You don't need a fancy program that requires a guy like me to come to your agency and tell you how I almost blew my brains out because of my former agency. Agencies need to understand that peer support isn't a check box, and just because you have it doesn't mean it's going to work.

Mental health programs within law enforcement need to be reinforced with assurance from the chief or sheriff that zero repercussions are going to occur if you come forward and ask for help.

Departments are still not grasping the concept that an epidemic is going on right now, and I'm not talking about COVID. I get emails still from officers asking about medication and counseling outside the department so they won't lose their job. All because departments have adopted this mentality that if you ask for mental health support that you're a danger to yourself and others. More importantly, these higher ups are worried about liability. Little do they know that by creating this culture, they have officers in some real bad shape not seeking mental health help they need.

On the flip side, you have bad players in our profession that cause such hostile work environments that good people are leaving due to the stress and aggravation.

The COVID-19 pandemic created a whole new mental health crisis for law enforcement. We have officers exposed to COVID with little to no direction from their agencies, and no personal protective equipment. This caused a lot of stress and anxiety for officers wondering what type of exposure they would be subjected to.

In my old department, before my departure, the health department was clueless about how to handle the pandemic and how to keep first responders protected. They were more concerned with citizens' medical history protection than first responders' health. This was extremely stressful and officers were understandably angry with the department and the city.

What made things worse during the pandemic was the failure of leadership within the department I left. The chief was absolutely clueless and lacked the experience to facilitate PPE. The worst part was the lack of compassion for line officers and disregard for their personal safety.

COVID was a perfect opportunity for departments to utilize and bolster mental health services for officers and family. Instead, they resorted to a dictatorship by telling officers, "Suck it up, this is the job." We lost a lot of really great new officers, and worse, we lost seasoned officers with less than 20 years on the job to non-law enforcement career. A lot of them could deal with the anti-cop movement and the radicals trying to defund the police, but the final straw was working for an agency that's incompetent and cares nothing about the officers' safety and mental health.

The public wants safe streets, safe schools, and to be able to walk down the street without being punched in the face, but they don't want force and they don't want to hear officers tell it as it is. The reality of it is that officers have had enough and have said, "Fuck it, this isn't worth it." The thin blue line is so thin that the boarder of order and chaos is grey.

Mental health in law enforcement is going in a direction that will cost healthcare companies and municipalities millions of dollars, because they fail to address problems head on. States are fighting vigorously to not allow PTSD care for first responders as a workers compensation injury, and Social Security won't even touch PTSD for first responders because it's part of the job. So after you survive the poor leadership within law enforcement, witness things no one should see, and do 20-25 years in law enforcement, you can't even collect any medical assistance from the state or the federal government. But if you're 700 pounds and ate yourself onto "My 600 Pound Life," you get to suck off the government's tit for as long as your buffalo inflated heart holds out. Some bullshit, right?

Mental health continues to be used as a weapon by agencies to discredit someone or justify their poor leadership. In my old agency, after I filed an FOIA request for my security clearance background investigation for my current employer, I was shocked to see what a sergeant in internal investigations wrote about me. This sergeant wrote, "I have concerns over the subject's mental or emotional stability because of how this whole thing played out in the public. It seemed like the subject just melted down. The subject also attempted suicide around 2019." Aside from this being retaliation, its highly illegal to say this to a potential employer let alone during a federal security clearance investigation.

This is a member (a sergeant) of the Alexandria City Police Departments Internal Investigations unit willingly and knowingly writing false information, and intentionally trying to prevent me from gaining future employment. If you read that over again, the worst part is my suicide attempt was in the spring of 2019, and I was working for the department and just got rehired after passing a full phycological exam.

Law enforcement agencies absolutely hate when you speak out publicly about their disfunction and shortcomings. They absolutely hated the fact that I wouldn't allow them to just toss me aside like trash and that I held them to the fire in the public. They couldn't take legal action against my first book because like this book, everything was factual with documentation. Agencies like the Alexandria City Police Department bully officers into staying quiet and disappearing. That wasn't happening after what they put me through. I wasn't nor will I stay quiet when it comes to treating people like shit and abusing your authority as a law enforcement agency.

The agency I'm currently with showed compassion and questioned my old departments motives and discredited what was written in my background investigation. My investigator actually told me, "I've been doing this for over 20 years and I've never seen any agency come after someone with this much vicious hate. We did a complete background check and found nothing that this sergeant wrote truthful. His statements solidified our conclusion that you had a public forum (podcast, YouTube channel, and best-selling book) and they didn't like that you spoke poorly of them."

This was comforting because I read that short clip out of the three pages the sergeant wrote and it discouraged me a little because it makes you question if the juice was worth the squeeze. Was it worth losing everything for nothing? The answer to that is you reading this book. It's worth it because you're aware of how things go when you fight back. Police departments create these hostile environments and expect you to lay down and take it because that's how it is. Fuck that, that's unacceptable and not okay.

People like this sergeant need to be held accountable by every available means in the legal system. Likewise with agencies that employ people like him. That high horse needs to be taken down a few pegs by a jury of 12 people who we represent and don't tolerate that kind of misconduct.

The kicker of it all is that my old agency will brag all day long that they are transparent and that they care about their officers, but that's horse shit. If you can do what they've done or write what they did about someone that gave 15 years to the community, then you don't give a shit about that person or mental health, you're just a bully and an asshole.

CHAPTER 10

A spouse's battle with the blue line

By

Nicole Ruggiero

Let me start by saying there are two sides to every line. I have had the opportunity to see things from both sides.

To live as a LEO wife as well as be a LEO myself. That in itself is a whole other story which I'll save for another book. Having a loved one, a partner dedicate their life to public service while a true honor, filled heart with pride and a blessing can also be a dull razor to the skin except it slowly cuts the person you love up inside and out in the form of mental and physical exhaustion, poor health habits, sleep deprivation, missed holidays, anniversaries and birthdays, fights and long and lonely nights, weekends and sometimes days that are so long you sometimes you may not see the one you love for days. That's only the beginning...

The first few years are always the worst. That's what we are told from the get go. It's going to be hard at first but it will be worth it, just need to show them you're a company man and you and make a name for yourself. Some academy instructors will recommend a book to read or suggest therapy or social media groups for you to join for LEO spouses to band together for support etc… some are ok some are not.

More or less it's a place or group to bitch about loneliness and heartache or read about it and 9/10 times you feel worse than you did after you read about it or went. If you're lucky you feel better or you'll at least tell your partner you do. Most of the time you don't.

I'm just being honest, Forgive me as I laugh out loud, that is a very gray term once you are a LEO spouse. You will soon learn that being honest with how you feel or what's on your mind will become a point of contention, at least it was for me.

Each and every time I told Nick how I felt or suggested I did not agree with a choice he made or was about to make, or ones that would be detrimental to his career, our home, our life or our future and family it would spiral into a fight or an argument. I was accused of being ungrateful for his sacrifice and I had no idea what I was talking about. I was given the speech about how he was irreplaceable and how invaluable he was to the department and they were the ones he trusted. His friends and superiors would always have his back and I was the one that didn't support him or what he needed to do to get to the next level. There was always a next level, always another hoop to jump through to get to the next step in the career ladder.

The worst thing was watching his so called friends, his brothers and sisters use and manipulate him to get what they needed and rarely was it anything that would help or support my husband or our family. But that was a battle that I learned early on that I could never win. It went from us vs the world to me vs them, by them I mean his agency and the brothers and sisters that would never ever have his best interests or our families in mind. Thats how deep they go when they go all in. This career path is all or nothing.

I saw what that mentality did to my husband and our family and I would not let it do that to me. The moment I was hired as a Deputy Sheriff, I treated it as it was a job, like any other job, I gave it my all for 12.5 hours each night. The only difference was that I got paid to serve and protect and when I was off duty in fact I was off duty, there would be no answering phones or emails or doing training on my time off. I was fully committed to my job but I needed to treat it as such. If that wasn't good enough then oh well, my family would always have to come first and foremost, the job was secondary. My husband and our children and our family was the reason why I put the vest and gun belt on and threw myself into dangerous situations night after night.

I saw my husband give up 15 plus years of his life to his agency, 15 plus years of our life, the best years in fact of our life, all given up to an agency and its minions that took everything he gave them and the moment he lost his value and went from a shiny penny to a dirty one, threw him away without even thinking twice about it. I watched people that I watched give birth and babysat each others children and weddings and baby showers and birthdays all drop off without even a moment of hesitation.

All of the sudden my husband who took care of his people while he was a Sergeant, people he protected and cared for slowly stepped back and away from him and us and one by one became distant reminders of a life that once was. I watched leaders, my own sheriff included in the neighboring agency care more about using Nick and his skills and his connections for his own agenda, used me as a pawn in his political game.

At this point in our life I was mentally broken down and I was drowning emotionally. My entire life was being torn apart and all those groups I belonged to and all those "friends" we discussed earlier left me almost instantly and took 10 steps back and away from me, my husband, and our family. No one prepares you for that, no book and no psychiatrist can prepare you for the mental breakdown, emotional trauma or the repercussions of trusting these people that were so called brothers and sisters of the thin blue line.

First it's the academy, then field training, and then two years of probation. By then the one you love is three plus years in and is brainwashed to think that the dedication they have and the thought the agency can't function without them is heavily ingrained in their brains and they're hard wired to need the adrenaline rushes and dumps and they become necessary to survive and thrive and no amount of discussion can change their heart and mind.

They will turn on you slowly. "How dare you not support me"…and "They need me"… or "The job is who I am, I'm nothing without it"…That is what they don't tell you in the beginning, they fail to tell you that you will raise your children on your own, make up excuses to friends and family to why you can't get together, you will loose a tremendous amount of money allowing them to buy new toys to feel powerful and accomplished, you will hide that and the expenses from family and friends, you will giggle and laugh and smile and pretend that all is fine. Most of the time because the one you love is either always angry or irritated from sleep deprivation, court, use of force investigations or studying for the next process or they live in a constant state of paranoia and hyperventilate and you know that if you force a visit or trip to the mall that it will ensue a fight or piss them off so that it ruins your time off so you learn to not even bother to try.

They don't tell you that it will be a miracle if you can get a vacation in or a weekend away and if you have a career not as a LEO the likelihood of you getting time off together will need to be planned months in advance. Say goodbye to spontaneity. It will be hard to have quality time because at this point when your loved one is finally off duty or on vacation they are so tired from all the emotional baggage they carry that they won't want to do half of things you planned to do. You'll end up dissatisfied and disappointed and they will be irritated and it will spark a fight or piss you both off, let alone ruin the time with your family.

All of this because you love them, and you will be the dutiful spouse and suck it up because it's what is best for them and your family. You will have to sacrifice just as much as they do to hold together the fragile family and roots you have. You will be whatever the one you love needs you to be to help keep them together, to be the glue.

There are times you will want to give up and walk away, there are times that you will feel empty and hanging by your last thread. I urge you to hold on. It won't always be that way. Breathe deep and take it one patient step at a time. At the very center is love and support and your LEO needs you and needs that.

While it's never easy to deal with the ups and downs, some days you swim with the current other days against it, some days you may almost drown. Those days you need to swim your hardest back to shore and regroup for yourself, your family and your partner.

Most agencies will do a poor job identifying mental burnout or even offer counseling after exposure to significant trauma on duty. You're not a therapist by any means but you know the one you love and you need to listen to them during those critical times. You need to identify the signs the one you love is struggling with. You are a team. Giving up is easy, but love and compassion is eternal, and you can make or break the one you love. They need you to be the therapist, the lover, the fighter, and cheerleading them on while picking them up when they're down.

Noticing the signs that they may not even be aware they're not ok. They need you more than they know and more than the job itself although they'll think they're indestructible and indispensable, in all reality they're completely replaceable. That is something they may not come to reality to even digest that information or really understand until they're at the end of their mental rope.

I think I did a fairly good job supporting my husband and ensuring he had a home and a bed to come home to, meals on the table, arms to hold, shoulder to lean on. At least I tried. I loved him harder as he pushed me away. I refused to give up on him when he so easily gave up on himself.

For 15 years I sat in the sidelines watching the man I married 6 years before he became a cop slowly let go of himself, loose himself in a cause and an agenda that wasn't his but was the agency and its mission. I watched him suffer the wrath of terrible leaders using him and his experience and expertise to their advantage, I watched them use him until he no longer had anything left to use. All the hours and time unpaid to be on the phone and all the stress and the anguish when he was passed over for processes that he aced because he wasn't popular. He was the good guy the loyal one. Loyal to the command staff to a fault. I watched them take and take and take until all he had left was his love of the job and even then they took that from him on a dreary Monday afternoon.

When I became a Deputy in the same city things came full circle for me. I saw things on my side and I was able to forgive and appreciate the secluded and suspicious, hyper vigilant lifestyle I was forced to live for so long. It clicked. It made sense. He wasn't trying to hurt his family he was protecting them from outsiders. I began to do many of the same things I hated that he did myself because we choose this life of service.

There is good and bad out there. We need to keep our head on a swivel at all times to protect ourselves and our partners. I read a quote once "Police have become a catch all for the city's problems. We are expected to be psychologists, social workers and mediators, and we are only trained for one of those jobs..."

When I went through the academy I went through CIT, Crisis Intervention Training. It was eye opening for me. I saw signs in my husband that he wasn't ok. He had left his agency and cane back, like I said he was brainwashed to believe that's all he was and could be.

About 4 weeks before my academy graduation day I was coming home early from fire arms practice. I call Nick to let him know I got out early. Little did I know that call was literally life changing, I could tell he was not ok and he broke down when I asked him if he was ok and finally opened up to his trauma and what was going on inside his head. He was ready to end it all, he planned it out. That day I never spoke to anyone about but my husband. I kept it buried in the deepest part of my soul. I wanted to shield him and protect him from the Stigma of PTSD,

Depression and Anxiety and ADHD. All of which my husband was later diagnosed.

That Monday afternoon will forever remain engraved in my mind and in my heart, I drove home and drove beyond reckless to get home to him. There was no way anyone or anything would stop me from getting home to him, I kept him on the phone as I drove using my new emergency vehicle operations skills to my best ability to make it across three counties in record time. When I came in I hugged him, told him I loved him and we would get him help. He agreed and I could see the glimmer of hope return. I almost lost the man I loved and shared my life with to suicide. I can't even think about what would have happened had I not gone home early that day and picked up the phone to call him.

Love is that powerful as is compassion and understanding. It is vital with communication to any relationship but it's critical as a LEO spouse. Your love matters, listening matters. We need to accept that the ones we love will experience significant trauma and need to talk through it with either therapy or with someone they trust. I was very lucky in my 15 years as a LEO spouse my husband would tell me a lot of what was going on and that helped him decompress. Not all LEO wives are created equal. Some cannot handle those stories, some spouses carry the trauma quietly to shield the ones that cannot hear about it. Make no mistake if you can't listen you need to help them find an outlet that can and will. That's your choice and responsibility as a LEO spouse, but it is a critical tool that they need to ensure they know they are not alone, they need a resource to grieve for the situations that they cannot control and the lives they may not always be able to save. .

Once I completed my field training I went through many ups and downs within my agency. I had so much stress to the point I almost had a nervous breakdown within the first year. I hid a lot from my husband and our kids,

I would leave for work early to cry in my car in the 7/11 parking lot around the corner from my agency before roll call. I literally lost my attention to focus because I lived in a constant state of brain fog and could not focus on anything, some days I was ok at work other days I was a mess. I worked in a jail in confinement and I worked hard, I loved my team and my partners, my job was to get them home at the end of the tour and to ensure the inmates were safe. Some nights I could barely take care of myself. I was sinking into deep depression and sky high anxiety.

My job was mentally and emotionally draining to the point my body started to fail me. For years after graduation I struggled so bad I had to see my therapist 2-3 times a month and this last year I was prescribed the maximum dosage of Zoloft because my depression became a trigger for migraines. I had to take anxiety medication to work with me because my anxiety and paranoia was so bad that I stopped functioning as a normal adult, and if I didn't take it before roll call I would sob in the bathroom in a unit until I could force myself to calm down.

I literally burned myself out both physically and mentally. If I was sick and called out I literally would text and call my team to tell them I was sorry I had to call out. I was terrified that my work family would get hurt if I called out. But why did I have to apologize to anyone? If you're sick you're sick. That's what sick leave is for. What the hell was wrong with me? I literally broke down at that point and thought to myself... wow this is what Nick must have felt when he called out.

That fear and hyper vigilant dedication was part of the brainwashing. The fear of missing out, the fear of letting your team and supervisors down. It all clicked. It came full circle...

By this time when I realized it, I confided in my husband what I was thinking, what I was feeling and the anxiety and panic I had even driving into work and how truly unhappy I was, I felt like I had lost my identity, who I was and I couldn't do it anymore. I had too medicate to function. My emotions were so bad my psychiatrist told me if I continued the path I was on it would destroy me physically and mentally before the year was over.

After a discussion about my mental state, Nick and I took a long weekend trip to Magnolia Homes and fell in love with the idea of startling our own business. We always wanted to open a coffee shop. This was always a top retirement goal. That is how The Roll Call Room Cafe was born. A beautiful little gourmet coffee shop that saved both of our lives and our family. We found a new purpose.

We became a necessity during a global pandemic with love and support of the community in which we lived and served.

I couldn't be more proud of where we are today and where we are going. My wonderful husband is slowing becoming the man I married 22 years ago. I am becoming the me that I used to be. Our children take pride in our business and our sacrifice. We have found a life after Police work. It does exist. We have found better ways to open up and communicate with each other. We have learned to never leave your partner in a fire. We pick each other up when one of us falls behind. We enjoy the moments and the little things we used to take for granted.

The moral of this story is there is a life after police work. You just need to open your heart and mind and figure out what that is. Marriage is 50/50, it takes two partners that are committed to each other and willing to take on the wild ride of life together. Some days marriage is 70/30, that is the beauty in finding a partner that completes you, they pick you up and help you walk when you can't run.

Do what makes you happy. Not every journey will be the same. Not everyone will have a happy ending. But the point is to try. Communicate even when it's hard and uncomfortable, that's the best time to talk and listen and the most important time to connect.

Life is short and time is not on our side, live each day as if it is your last, treasure those moments because life is fragile. Remember the couples that go through everything that is meant to tear them apart can come out even stronger than they were before.

THE END